365 DAYS OF

mindful meditations

DAILY GUIDANCE FOR A CALMER, HAPPIER YOU

365 DAYS OF MINDFUL MEDITATIONS

An Hachette UK Company
www.hachette.co.uk

Vie Books, an imprint of Summersdale Publishers
Part of Octopus Publishing Group Limited
Carmelite House
50 Victoria Embankment
LONDON
EC4Y 0DZ
UK

www.summersdale.com

Printed and bound in China

ISBN: 978-1-80007-101-8

Substantial discounts on bulk quantities of Summersdale books are available to corporations, professional associations and other organizations. For details contact general enquiries: telephone: +44 (0) 1243 771107 or email: enquiries@summersdale.com.

To ....

From ....

introduction

A stressful and challenging lifestyle often gets in the way of self-care, but in a world that is more demanding than ever, it's time we understood that it is just as vital to look after our emotional welfare as our bodies.

Mindfulness is a practice that trains the brain to focus on the present moment. It helps to combat negative emotions by letting go of sadness or worries, and encourages compassion toward ourselves and others. Meditation, meanwhile, is a means of quietening the mind — teaching us to take stock of our thoughts and emotions without judgement. It can bring calm in challenging situations.

Each time you sit for a mindful meditation session, you activate the parasympathetic nervous system, which decreases your heart rate and lowers the release of stress hormones, adrenaline and cortisol. This helps combat insomnia, anxiety and lack of concentration – while boosting your mood and confidence. Research shows practising mindfulness and meditation can reduce stress, soothe feelings of anxiety and even tackles symptoms of depression. Being centred in your mind builds compassion toward others, allowing for healthier relationships. *365 Days of Mindful Meditations* offers simple exercises to build a calmer mind. With time and dedication you will feel this positive effect on your overall well-being.

january

Begin your mindfulness journey by starting a journal. Each morning, write down five things for which you feel grateful. They may be small reflections — such as the means to have a hot shower or waking up healthy. Even on your hardest days, delve deep to find those things, however trivial they seem. At night, glance over your list. This will start and end the day positively.

Begin the day with gentle yoga to wake your body. Lie on your back and bring your knees to your chest while inhaling and exhaling deeply. Hold for as long as possible.

Before you leave your bed, sit up comfortably and breathe in slowly through your nose and out, slowly, through your mouth. Inhale, exhale. Think only of your breath and how it feels. This is a form of mindful meditation. Repeat for two minutes, using a clock as a timer.

It is inevitable that your mind will wander while meditating. When you notice, gently divert the focus back to your breathing. Try to let go of any frustration and realize this is a natural part of meditation.

Our life is shaped by our mind; we become what we think.

GAUTAMA BUDDHA

There is no right or wrong in meditation. The more you practise, the more you will master a method that best suits you. In the meantime, relax and enjoy a few blissful minutes to yourself.

Practise your breathing meditation at the same time each day. A regular routine will bring you comfort. As you settle in, increase your meditation time in increments of two or five minutes. On days when you seek calm, allow your session to last for as long as is needed.

Stand in front of the mirror and see yourself in your entirety. Look yourself in the eye and remind yourself five times, "I am worthy. I am deserving. I am enough."

Should you feel your shoulders slump during meditation, slowly lift and straighten your spine. Do this as many times as necessary during your session. This will prevent backache and soreness in the neck.

•••（10）•••

There are three solutions to every problem: acceptance, change and acknowledgement followed by tolerance. If you cannot accept the problem, then change it. If you cannot change it, then acknowledge its impact before letting it be.

Create a corner of calm in a quiet part of your home. Enhance it with dim lighting, comforting blankets and rugs, photos, inspiring books, organic scented oils or candles – whatever creates a sense of security. If possible, make this a non-working environment, and let this be your place of peace.

••• 12 •••

Feeling irritated or restless is natural when starting out with mindful meditation. Instead of fighting those emotions, acknowledge them and allow them to pass. In time, you will find these feelings become much less prominent.

As you start your day, practise mindfulness by becoming aware of your movements. Feel the sensations of simply "being". Pause, sit down for a while, take a few deep breaths.

Use your journal to note down any strong thoughts and emotions. Before bed, reflect on them. Find joy in your positive feelings. Dissect feelings of discomfort.

Mindfulness isn't difficult, we just need to remember to do it.

SHARON SALZBERG

If you are having a challenging day when perhaps you feel emotionally overwhelmed or things aren't going to plan, try to let go of frustration and annoyance. Understand that struggle is a part of the human condition. Not every day can feel perfect, and that's okay.

The keys to successful practice are comfort and alertness. You don't need to sit in the lotus position unless you so wish – simply maintain a straight spine to help your lungs fill deeply with oxygen. This alignment also prevents soreness in the back, neck and shoulders over time.

• • • • • •

For just a few moments, take a step outside into the cold without a jacket. Focus on your blood vessels as they begin to constrict with your warm blood. Your extremities may begin to tingle. Feel every single sensation as if you are feeling it for the first time. You are alive. Your body is a miracle. You have a life to live.

• • • 19 • • •

If you shut your eyes tightly while meditating it will tense your facial muscles. Instead, allow your eyelids to rest gently in the closed position.

Remind yourself to practise mindfulness by leaving inspirational tools in plain sight. For example, keep a cushion for meditation in the middle of the room, leave candles in your preferred place of calm or place a rolled-out yoga mat ready for your next session.

••• (21) •••

Compassion is infectious. Smile at the faces you pass on the street, hold doors open for a little longer and say an extra loud "hello" to those who catch your eye. Your kindness will reflect inwards as well as out to the world and provide you with noticeable beauty in the present moment.

••• (22) •••

After each meditation session, take time to acknowledge how you feel emotionally and physically. Ask yourself: "Is my mind clearer? Am I feeling calmer?" If not, how do you feel? By establishing an understanding between your mindful meditation practice and how you feel afterwards, you will be able to adapt your exercises to suit you — and appreciate the benefits of your self-care.

••• (23) •••

Nothing can cure the soul but the senses, just as nothing can cure the senses but the soul.

OSCAR WILDE

●●● ●●●

Life is brimming with humble tasks. We eat, drink, shower, walk, water our plants. Practise being mindful as you carry these out. Imagine it's your first time; listen to the sounds, breathe in the smells. Your life is rich enough to be able to do these simple, beautiful things — savour every moment.

●●● (25) ●●●

If you have missed a meditation session, make a note in your journal about why. By writing down your reasons, you are accepting accountability and will feel less guilt. Tomorrow you can start afresh.

●●● 26 ●●●

Your self-care experience is unique to you and cannot be compared to the experiences of others. Do not judge or analyze your sessions into "good" or "bad" experiences — or get too caught up in negotiating the well-being-related vocabulary used in magazines or television shows. Simply practise regularly, with dedication, and follow the exercises that naturally work for you.

27

Meditation is not a means
to an end. It is both the
means and the end.

JIDDU KRISHNAMURTI

Take a walk at a natural pace. Place your hands where you feel comfortable. Focus on the rise and fall of your feet. Feel the movement in your leg muscles, how your body sways as you walk. Remain aware and safe in your environment — but keep returning your focus to the sensation of walking.

Call a loved one who you haven't contacted for a while. Show them you have time for them by speaking on the phone rather than messaging.

••• •••

Note down five things you have done out of kindness this month. They may consist of physical acts, emotional support or other contributions toward yourself or others. Take pride in those actions and dare to smile at the goodness within you. You are making a difference.

••• •••

Feelings, whether of compassion or irritation, should be welcomed, recognized, and treated on an absolutely equal basis, because both are ourselves.

THÍCH NHẤT HẠNH

february

Practise being in the moment through mindfulness within your home. You can do this by being alert to the sights, sounds, smells and textures that surround you. If you open a window, stop to feel the fresh air against your face. As you open your curtains, feel the fabric against your hands. Listen to the creaking floorboards with each step and take in the deep scent of your shampoo as you shower.

Gently lower your chin toward your chest to release tension in your neck. Inhale, exhale. Slowly move your head to the left and breathe. Do the same to the right.

If you are happy to embrace change, vary where you practise your mindful meditation. Find a quiet spot on a park bench, or a new path to walk.

••• (04) •••

Follow your intuition. That instinct you feel, deep inside, knows what is best for both your mind and body — even if the actioning isn't easy to follow.

**The horizon leans forward,
Offering you space to place
new steps of change.**

MAYA ANGELOU

••• (06) •••

Roll your shoulders back, straighten your spine and pull your shoulder blades down towards your lower back. Feel your back muscles as they stretch. Keep your chest lifted as you breathe in, and out, deeply and fully. Help yourself to feel physically well each day.

••• (07) •••

Namaste is a Sanskrit greeting that means "the light in me greets the light in you". Say a silent *namaste* to every person you interact with; see beyond their dress, their expressions and their names. Be open to their soul.

••• (08) •••

Show compassion in how you speak to yourself. This may, at times, require active intervention, where you stop, rethink and rephrase your internal commands. Swap "I've failed" for "I gave it my best"; "I give up, this is too hard" for "this is tough, but I'll keep trying" and "I don't know how to..." to "I must learn to..."

••• (09) •••

The calendar year showcases cycles of endings and new beginnings. This is the beauty of life. Observe the bare branches of the trees and acknowledge that, in a few short months, they will be full of life.

Making your bed in the morning helps the transition from a place of sleep into the waking world. By doing this small task, you are giving yourself time to prepare for the day ahead.

Choose to switch off your television and spend your evening with an alternative source of entertainment. Read a book, have an in-person conversation, take a long hot bubble bath, or spill your thoughts and emotions onto the pages of your journal.

••• (12) •••

Savour your final meal of the day. Place your knife and fork down between mouthfuls and indulge in the simple flavours you are tasting. Allow your tongue to trace the textures of the ingredients. Swallow small portions to allow your body to digest slowly. Breathe in the aromas from your dish. Savour the taste. Can you smell the herbs? Can you identify the spices?

••• (13) •••

In the end, just three things matter: how well we have lived. How well we have loved. How well we have learned to let go.

JACK KORNFIELD

This morning, send a message to someone dear to say "I love you". Say it with meaning and imagine their face as they open the message. Let the love bubble inside you as you continue your day.

••• (15) •••

The palms of our hands are particularly sensitive. Nourish your energy flow by dropping your arms against your legs with your palms facing up toward to sky. Spread your fingers wide and apart. Feel the stretch in your palms. Hold that stretch for three long breaths, in and out.

Work with what makes you most comfortable while meditating. Place cushions under your knees if you sit cross-legged or place a pillow behind you if your lower back needs more stability.

17

Take one simple step toward decluttering your living space. Start with the humble task of washing up your dishes as you use them, instead of leaving them in the sink.

18

The world would be a dull place if we were all the same. Avoid making comparisons between yourself and others – this only works to take away your peace of mind.

Retrain your destructive thoughts to become constructive. If a busy schedule is leaving you feeling overwhelmed, use the following mantra to give your mind focus: "I have all the time I need." Repeat this phrase out loud every time your mind fills with worry, reaffirming how it is you would like to feel.

Find time for the people and things you love, including yourself. Being alone and feeling lonely do not equate to the same thing. There is so much joy to be found in having time for you.

••• 21 •••

Say "no" more often. Remind yourself that you are able to use this powerful word freely and unapologetically for your own well-being. Repeat it in the mirror, until it flows off your tongue with confidence. Allow it to become second nature. Once you feel comfortable saying it without fear, "no" can be liberating beyond measure. This single word can set you free from toxic situations and relationships.

Oh how beautifully you
have grown in courage since
February of last year.

MORGAN HARPER NICHOLS

Recognize that true happiness isn't something coming to you in the future. It's here with you now. It's in the small things you do and experience every day – like enjoying your favourite breakfast, a call from a friend, the warm hug of someone you love dearly. Happiness is all around you. Can you feel it?

•••(24)•••

Write down three things that went well today, identifying the causes of those positives. Your achievements are now written in black and white – soak them in from the page.

Making space for sadness is just as important as valuing happiness. Instead of burying your sadness and being ashamed, acknowledge how you feel, question where it comes from and write these thoughts down in your journal. Let your notes be your outlet.

As a new month draws near, reflect on the habits you hope to lose with the darkness of winter. Note them down as a reminder to let them go as the days go on.

We need to do a better job of putting ourselves higher on our own "to-do" list.

MICHELLE OBAMA

While you drive or take public transport today, pay attention to the way you are sitting. Relax your shoulders and head, unclench your hands and jaw, stretch your spine and neck.

Make today special and full of self-love — because 29 February only features in our calendar once every four years. Start with your regular stretches and breathing exercises and follow it up by immersing in nature. Laugh if you can, cry if you need to and, at the end the day, remind yourself of your reasons to be grateful.

march

Yoga and mindful meditation share similar goals of emotional and physical peace. While yoga uses body movements, mindfulness and meditation typically involve quiet contemplation. *Shavasana* is the resting or "corpse" pose and is practised at the end of a yoga session. It involves lying on your back with your eyes closed, breathing deeply — maintaining awareness of your breath. Take this position if you are craving calm.

Shake out your arms and legs and let tense muscles loosen. Feel your body relax from your head and neck to your fingers and all the way through to your toes.

Go for a walk to celebrate the days getting lighter. Can you see the first signs of spring around you? Are the birds singing? Which colours have appeared since your last walk? Take your journal and note down the signs of nature you see and hear.

• • • (04) • • •

Open your windows to let in the fresh air. Feel the breeze cleanse your surroundings. Allow any stale energy to dissipate. Let the light flow through your home, brightening up your space and your mind.

Give your body the vital fuel that it needs in abundance — water. Drink plenty of fluid daily — not only to keep your skin supple, your hair glossy and your eyes revitalized, but so that your body and mind stay alert and function optimally. Feel the difference in your body within just a few days.

06

Remember: no matter how grey the day, the sky is still blue above the clouds. Spring is coming.

07

Mindfulness is the aware, balanced acceptance of the present experience. It isn't more complicated than that.

SYLVIA BOORSTEIN

Finding the right exercise for you can help your emotional and physical well-being. Trial different options to find what you enjoy most. Research suggests just 20 minutes of exercise can improve your mood for 12 hours, by triggering the release of chemical endorphins and dopamine in the body, which reduce the production of stress hormones, cortisol and adrenaline.

Plant daffodil or crocus bulbs in a pot by your window and allow the light to stream in. Watch as new life begins to sprout.

Keep viewing your mindful meditation exercises as an everyday practice. They are becoming a part of who you are.

Try acting from a place of compassion today. If you feel annoyed by someone, ask yourself why they may have said or done what they did. Try to find understanding toward their thinking and position.

You need to learn to how to select your thoughts just the same way you select your clothes every day.

ELIZABETH GILBERT

Be a friend to yourself. Through mindful meditation, you are getting to know who you are deep down; welcome your findings with warmth rather than criticism.

Dance. Do it in your front room, kitchen or garden – anywhere where you have space. Dance to the music that brings back your favourite memories; those that encompass happiness, friendship and freedom. Feel the movement in each part of your body; in your arms as they swing and your legs as they glide and absorb each beat.

Lend a nod to World Sleep Day (the third Friday in March) by allowing yourself an early night. Crawl into the comfort of your bed and read through your gratitude list. Then melt into the pillows with a good book. As your eyelids droop, let go into a peaceful sleep.

If you haven't practised yoga for a while, now is the time to get back to it. Lay down on your mat and enjoy how well your body responds to stretches.

••• 17 •••

I... take a few deep breaths and set my intentions for the day.

ARIANA HUFFINGTON

If you are feeling nervous or worried about an upcoming event or situation, use the following affirmation to give your mind focus: "I can do this. I am ready." By repeating this phrase out loud every time you feel fear, you are reaffirming how it is you would like to feel.

Focus on completing one task at a time from your to-do list. Avoid the stress of tackling too many projects at once and allow yourself the gratification of ticking off each task from your list as a job well done.

Today is the Spring Equinox. Say a final farewell to the habits and routine you wish to leave behind and embrace the new beginnings stirring inside you. Allow yourself to start afresh on anything — and everything — you wish to change.

Swap uptight and uncomfortable clothing for outfits that make you feel confident, secure and relaxed. Compromise, where necessary — even on workwear — to allow you to feel like yourself. Only settle when you are at ease with your choices.

"Sound bathing" is an ancient Tibetan practice of lying in a dimly lit room, listening to soothing sounds created from specially made metal and crystal bowls. Research suggests the sounds calm us and reduce any stress we may feel. Invest in an app, or playlist, and enjoy this practice once a week.

A short run can work wonders for your mind — thanks to the increased flow of oxygenated blood to the brain. Savour every long, deep breath and each leg muscle movement; feel the life seep back into you.

Project who you would like to be. If you lack confidence, stand with your head held high, chest pushed out and hands on hips.

Try to wake up without an alarm. Waking naturally helps you feel fresh and alert.

There's an awareness behind your fear. There's an awareness behind your desire.

RUSSELL BRAND

Find joy in creating something new. Bake a cake, sketch out a drawing, practise your cross-stitching, cook a dish you've never tried before, paint! Lose yourself in the beauty of the creative process and in a new challenge.

●●● 28 ●●●

It's the perfect time of year for gardening. Create a small vegetable patch, either in boxes or planted in the ground. Plant seeds or saplings that flower in late spring and summer, such as aubergine, peppers and green beans. Water them and watch them grow.

••• **29** •••

Consider making small, mindful changes when shopping for new clothes. Always ask yourself: "Do I love it? Will I wear it often? Am I comfortable?" before buying.

••• **30** •••

Slow down. Place your hand over your heart for one minute and feel each beat. Remind yourself that you are alive and the day is yours.

••• **31** •••

When you take the time and space you need, kindly and responsibly, you're suddenly available to the people you love in a whole new way.

LENA DUNHAM

april

01

By keeping up your regular meditation session, you can learn to manage emotions as they arise, allowing you to respond with consideration and wisdom to each situation. In ancient times, humans often reacted to threats such as wild bear attacks or tribal wars. Today, we have very different threats — work deadlines, arguments and other unpleasantries, so keeping perspective on our internal reaction is important.

02

Breathe deeply. You can practise deepening your breath while in *Shavasana* (the resting pose) by placing your hands on your stomach, feeling your rib cage rise and fall.

Take a long walk around a nearby park. As you enter, take a deep breath of fresh air and let it out slowly. Turn your phone on silent and take time to listen to the breeze among the leaves. Watch the light filtering through the trees. Isn't nature wonderful?

As rumbling rainclouds gradually give way to sunshine, look out for rainbows. They are out there, and they are beautiful.

Precious moments [are] when I can have a quick walk in nature.

JANE GOODALL

Once a season, go through your wardrobe and take out any items you haven't worn. If they are in good condition, place them in a bag ready to be taken to your nearest thrift store.

• • • (07) • • •

Reach out to a family member or friend. Staying in contact with loved ones helps reassert the support that surrounds you. If you can't chat in person, arrange for a phone or video call. Not only does this help combat feelings of isolation, but it is also a reminder that you are loved, wanted and needed.

Sit with a straight posture and relaxed shoulders. As your breathing slows, focus on the tense parts of your body and, one at a time, give each part permission to relax. Take slow, deep breaths as you do so, saying the words "let" as you inhale, and "go" as you exhale. Repeat for as long as needed.

Give yourself permission to be inaccessible sometimes. Leave messages unread, emails unanswered, turn off your phone. It's perfectly okay to take time away from communicating.

Plant a tree — either in your own garden or in a public space. For the latter, there are community groups who arrange planting sessions. As you sprinkle water over the sapling, think carefully about the life you have given rise to. Trees help living things survive, including you. Your work is invaluable.

Respond, rather than react, to the behaviour of others. The difference between the two is choice. When you react to a situation, you allow the other person's actions to control your emotions. If you respond, you can be considered, protect boundaries and choose the best course of action.

Before you get out of bed, make your first thoughts about the day ahead: what do you want to achieve today? What is on your to-do list? Go forth into your day with a purpose.

Finding peace doesn't mean being in a place where there is no noise, no hard work or challenges. It means being able to live through all of those things and still feel the calm in your mind. Regular mindful meditation practise will help achieve this.

Before you speak, let your words pass through three gates: is it true? Is it necessary? Is it kind?

RUMI

When you view your life as a blessing, it will feel like one. Start today.

Positive affirmations work by turning negative inner whispers into positive inner life coaching. Plant pictures of your dreams in your imagination and water them daily with positive thoughts. "I am worthy. I am capable. I can achieve this." Of course, take practical steps toward your goals through study and work, too — but you can encourage your self-belief by repeating these affirmations.

Spread out your food intake by eating small amounts more often, rather than three large meals. If you're peckish, have nutritious snacks ready, such as sliced fruit or vegetables, nuts or a smoothie. This will level out your blood sugar and help prevent tiredness and low moods.

Be happy to work on yourself, by yourself, for yourself.

I meditate in the morning. For me, training is also my meditation.

DWAYNE JOHNSON

Try to eat mindfully. Slowly place each spoonful in your mouth. Be quietly aware of how fortunate you are to have food on your plate.

Understand that the more you try to control a situation, the more it has control of you. Believe that only good can come of nature taking its own course — and give the world permission to unfold how it sees best. Free yourself of distress and worry.

• • • (22) • • •

Take a few minutes to sit comfortably, placing a hand on your heart. Feel your breath going into your chest and slowly seeping out. You are connecting your mind and heart – and redirecting your focus to your lifeline.

• • • (23) • • •

Contentment can be found in the present. Stop counting the weeks until your next holiday. Stop rushing through the day because you wish to get home. Take pride in this very moment – because once it is gone, you will never have it again.

• • • (24) • • •

A thought is a thought, not a prophecy. Remember, you are not your thoughts.

Life is rarely straightforward for anyone. Everyone you meet is fighting their own battles. Take comfort in the fact you are not alone in your struggles. Solutions come by taking one step at a time.

·· • (26) • ··

Sit for two minutes and focus on your heartbeat. As thoughts enter your mind — positive or negative — allow them to stay for a few seconds before passing.

·· • (27) • ··

Accept the apology you never got. Once you find it in you to do this, you will immediately feel lighter.

28

Discover the scents that relax you. Lavender, sage and cinnamon help with calming. Invest in candles or essential oils to cleanse your surroundings, then sit for a few minutes absorbing the smell.

29

You have nearly completed four months of guided self-care. Reward your progress with activities you love — perhaps time with friends, your favourite takeaway or a hot bath.

30

The reason why I meditate and pray in general is just to remind myself that it is not about me.

MACKLEMORE

may

Choose the best mindful meditation practice to suit your needs at a particular time. *Calming* meditation – such as breathing and sensation-experiencing exercises or repeating affirmations and mantras – typically involves concentrating on a particular asset to quiet the mind when anxious or overwhelmed. *Insight* meditation manages thoughts and emotions in a gentle manner and helps to process negative feelings. On days when you are feeling yourself, return to a mix of both.

Stimulate blood flow in your legs, ankles and feet by lying back with a small pillow or rolled towel underneath your knees. Breathe, long and deep.

●●● ●●●

Remind yourself why you are investing your time in mindful meditation by writing down how you have benefited from the process so far. Refer back to these notes regularly to keep yourself on track.

●●● (04) ●●●

Find a book that inspires you. It can be about anything — a biography, an educational tool or a fictional story. Read one chapter and lose yourself in another world. By choosing something enlightening or passionate, you will encourage empowerment within you, too.

● ● ● (05) ● ● ●

Use your journal to identify a problem you are facing. Describe the issue in detail and be as specific as possible. Then outline, in writing, the possible solutions. For each solution, note the pros and cons before highlighting the best outcome. This form of insight meditation is the first step in solving the issue.

● ● ● (06) ● ● ●

A comforting touch can soothe anxiety and initiate security. Reaching out to someone you care for can help you feel safe. Ask for a hug. Hold a hand. Look them in the eye. Everything is okay.

Spritz your meditation cushions with a mix of water and tea tree or lemongrass essence to add a natural scent to your space.

Empathy comes with kindness and compassion for others. Ask loved ones who are facing challenges questions such as: "What has this been like for you?" and "Are you okay?"

If you know how to worry, you know how to meditate. It means to think of something over and over.

JOYCE MEYER

World Meditation Day occurs in mid to late May each year. Give thanks to the power of your mindful meditation experiences by spending the day in a simple sensory state. Before each action or activity, each meal or drink, take a few minutes to listen, feel, taste and smell. How wonderful it is to be able to notice the little things.

Notice how your communication skills are developing. By focusing attention on the current moment, you are naturally engaging more and hearing what those around you have to say. These small adjustments are allowing your connections to blossom.

••• (12) •••

Stress and worry come from thinking too much about the future. Regret, resentment and sadness come from the inability to move on from the past. Remove that negativity by being mindful, in the present.

••• (13) •••

Disappointment is a part of life. Once you accept this, you will see life differently.

••• (14) •••

Make a hot drink. Savour every mouth-watering sip without distractions. Feel the warmth as you wrap your hands around the mug, the soothing sensation as it trickles down your throat and the warming deep in your stomach.

Think of a time you felt safe, comfortable and cherished. It may have seemed insignificant at the time, but when you remember that moment, perhaps you are still filled with reassurance, relief, contentment or affection. Describe how it makes you feel in your journal.

If you feel anxious, overwhelmed or low, think of a moment when you felt safe, comforted and loved. Close your eyes and lose yourself in the emotion that went through your head that day. Breathe deeply, in and out, as you think of it. Continue for as long as it feels right.

Talking therapy isn't only meant for sessions with a counsellor. Talking to friends and family is also important and necessary. Speak honestly and openly to someone you trust about something that is bothering you — it can be liberating.

Create a self-care plan. Start by making a list in your journal of the key exercises you wish to practise and why. A goal can be helpful in targeting the issues causing you the most pain.

Enjoy the little things in life because one day you'll look back and realize they were the big things.

KURT VONNEGUT JR

Feeling overwhelmed can be a natural part of life. Start with deep breathing exercises to calm your heart and mind. Once your breathing has slowed to a natural pace, write a list of what can be controlled in this situation and what cannot be controlled. Focus on what you can control.

Intuition is wisdom that comes from deep within your body. It's the most reliable compass we have. Learn to trust your inner instinct; it knows where you need to be.

Life happens, and that is okay. When an event occurs, try to acknowledge it without thinking further about its positive or negative connotations. Tell yourself, "It happened, and I accept that."

Stop rushing through your day. You may be pleasantly surprised at how much more you have time for.

••• 24 •••

With every setback comes opportunity. Rather than associate disappointment with failure, link it with "chance". This is your chance to create a new and exciting path.

Allow yoga to stretch out the discomfort in your body. Lower yourself to the ground to rest on your hands and knees and inhale as you stretch your tailbone toward the sky. As you exhale, slowly lower your buttocks toward your heels and bring your forehead toward the ground. Align your arms by your sides, then gently reach out in front of you. Feel the deep stretch.

••• 26 •••

Write affirmations and mantras on the positive outcome you are seeking and say them out loud in the present tense. For example, "I will move to the next level of my career this year."

Assess your self-care practice. Are you taking enough time to focus on you? Self-care is a necessary tool for a healthy, productive and happy life.

Repeat this mantra whenever you feel overcome by anxiety: "I am present, and I am safe." Take deep breaths, in and out, each time you say it.

Until you make peace with who you are, you'll never be content with what you have.

DORIS MORTMAN

The calmness you find within your short meditation sessions is always within you. The more you practise and achieve that calm, the more these exercises will aid you during challenging times. Gradually increasing the time spent on your meditation and mindfulness sessions each day allows peace and self-awareness to grow, too. Aim to now practise for 15 to 20 minutes each day. This is an ongoing journey you have embarked on.

[Meditation] really helps create not only a sense of balance... but serenity and kind of calm state of mind.

EVA MENDES

june

Sing. Whether it's at home alone or with a choir, just sing from the heart. Projecting your voice is a wonderful way to release any pent-up frustrations. Singing allows you to exercise the lungs with longer, deeper breaths – helping your heart rate to slow and your heart to pump fresh oxygenated blood around your body. Plus, singing along to much-loved melodies and harmonies is comforting.

Sit straight with your legs stretched out in front of you. Inhale, keeping your buttocks connected fully with the floor. Exhale, placing your palms on the ground, and push up with your spine.

Take small steps to declutter your space. When you take a break from work, clear away something from your desk. Before you close down your computer, clear your desktop. Recycle any papers you no longer need. By reducing chaos, your mind will also feel lighter and less chaotic.

Do you have a hobby you have lost touch with? If so, consider signing up to a local club that celebrates that activity. Communities often hold wonderful get-togethers, such as book clubs or gardening groups. This is a great way to make new friends with similar interests and focus your mind toward calming activities.

You are free to decide whether your anxiety is warranted. Anxiety is your body's way of alerting you to danger. However, in some situations perhaps the perceived threat isn't as harmful as it seems.

••• 06 •••

Start the day by repeating this mantra ten times in the mirror: "My life has unlimited possibilities."

There is nothing either good or bad, but thinking makes it so...

WILLIAM SHAKESPEARE

Mindful meditation can be practised anywhere. At home, on a train, in the park, at your desk and even as you are walking. Use the skills you have learned whenever you need them, regardless of where you are.

Focus on the rhythm of your walk: left foot, right foot, left foot, right foot.

••• (10) •••

If you have skipped a few days of meditation, don't worry — the mind is like a muscle. You will soon find your peace once you resume your routine.

● ● ● (11) ● ● ●

If you suffer from upper body tension, begin your mindful meditation session by focusing on your neck and shoulders. Inhale and count to ten slowly, while squeezing and relaxing your muscles. Repeat this technique until you find you are relaxed.

● ● ● (12) ● ● ●

As the summer sun rises, open all your windows to allow the fresh air to filter through your home. Bask in the warmth and light of a beautiful summer day. Allow the revitalized air to swirl around your belongings and cleanse the atmosphere.

Relax your body with a deep sigh. Breathe in fully and breathe out for longer. This deep exhalation can release built-up tension and help reset your muscles.

●●● (14) ●●●

If you are particularly enjoying yoga-based self-care, invest in a guided programme — there are plenty of complimentary classes available on YouTube — where you can maximize your practice.

Much of... life is self-acceptance, maybe all of it.

JACK KORNFIELD

Make a conscious effort to slow down, no matter what your day has in store. When we move at a fast pace, our mind naturally quickens to keep up with our physical step. Even the smallest adaption can help, and as your energy relaxes, so will your body. You will now be moving in a peaceful yet more purposeful stride, and your mind can be calm in its thoughts.

Buy yourself flowers. Place the vase somewhere you will see it all day.

Treat yourself to a well-being hour, just because you can. Choose a massage, manicure, food scrub or something else you will enjoy and tell yourself, "I deserve this." Close your eyes while you experience the sensations; the warming touch, the bristles against your feet.

Find peace in spending time alone. While staying busy might help keep your mind away from worries, having time to yourself is also precious. Spend those moments doing an activity that soothes your soul, like listening to your favourite album or reading a magazine you enjoy.

Moving on from any difficult situation is rarely a smooth process. Often, you will find yourself taking two steps forward and one step back. That's okay. Accept that it is a matter of time.

On the longest day of the year, take a mindful walk. Let your mind be bedazzled by the world around you.

Meditation showed me how much energy silence has.

MADONNA

Self-esteem can be brutally affected by negative thoughts infiltrating your mind. By learning to let those thoughts to pass, rather than impact the stability and peace of your mind, you can prevent fluctuation in moods and the loss of your self-esteem. Imagine your thoughts as clouds passing overhead. They don't linger long, and gradually disappear into the distance.

Endeavour to prioritize kindness toward yourself. Just a few words of self-encouragement can make a big difference. Look in the mirror with compassionate eyes and tell yourself, "You are doing so well. I love you."

Go for a swim. Swimming is a wonderful full-body workout that also allows your muscles to relax and unwind. Breathing patterns and repetitive arm strokes encourage focus, while the sensation of the water against your body introduces a sense of calm.

Picture yourself overcoming hurdles; perhaps ones of sadness, hurt or anger. Imagine your face glowing in the warm sunshine as you leap over each one, embracing the freedom and boundless path ahead of you. Visualize this when you feel low, knowing you will reach that road again soon.

With a little encouragement and support, your mind has tremendous power. Believe in it and you. You can achieve great things when starting from a belief that it can happen. Even if your challenges feel like mountains, it is that positive, tucked away mindset that will push you to begin the climb.

Get comfortable with feeling uncomfortable — because sitting with your feelings is one of the purest processes of mindful meditation. Rather than resist your discomfort, welcome it, give it space to expand and then leave your mind.

Congratulations, you have reached six months of mindful meditation. Use your journal to write a list of the benefits you have personally experienced from your sessions and make a note of how you feel your thoughts have evolved over the last few months.

The truth is, of course, that what one calls the interruptions are precisely one's real life.

C. S. LEWIS

july

01

Try to find forgiveness toward someone who has hurt you. Sit with your eyes closed and breathe slowly, then picture someone for whom you feel abundant love. Imagine their love, and visualize your love for them, as a bright light. Feel the warmth in that visualisation. Now repeat the exercise with someone you hold negative feelings toward. Be patient, keep offering them light.

02

Stretch your chest muscles by lying on your front and adopting the Sphinx pose. Keep your forearms flat on the ground, your elbows tucked under your shoulders and inhale as you lift your upper body.

Naps can increase alertness, enhance moods and improve memory, and are a healthier alternative to caffeine and sugar. So set an alarm for 20 minutes and power up!

Write a list of the values that make you a kind person. Read through each one carefully, taking in just how much goodness you have within you. Be proud of the person you are today.

How we spend our days is, of course, how we spend our lives.

ANNIE DILLARD

Switch your phone and television off at least an hour before you go to bed. Screens and the activities they enable naturally keep your mind active. By switching off some time before bed, you are allowing your mind to wind down naturally, providing a sense of calm in preparation for a peaceful sleep.

••• (07) •••

Talk to friends about your mindful meditation journey. Do you know someone who also practises? If so, share your experiences with them, ask them about theirs. By discussing your journeys without comparing, you will inspire each other to stay dedicated and motivated.

••• **08** •••

If you find yourself in a confrontational situation, use the skills you are learning through meditation, from self-calming to compassion toward others, to aid how you handle it.

••• **09** •••

Try something new today; take an alternative route home, try somewhere new for lunch or cook yourself an unusual dinner.

••• **10** •••

I visualize what I want through meditation. The process of meditating is a great way of making sure I have my priorities sorted.

SHILPA SHETTY

Try colouring in. Invest in a mindfulness colouring book that contains pages of various shapes and pictures. Spend an hour focusing on the sensation of your pencils against the paper and watching the colour spread as it fills the page.

Have you been meditating each day? Tick off your progress in your diary. Everything changes; such is the nature of life. However, maintaining your meditation routine each day will ground you. It is your constant.

●●● (13) ●●●

Place a vase full of blooming sunflowers near your bed. Observe and appreciate the brightness of summer over the next few days.

Arrange an evening playing board or card games with your housemates, friends or family.

While driving, focus on the comfort of your seated position. As you reach a red traffic light, stretch out your spine by sitting straight, put one or both feet firmly in the footwell and push your arms against the steering wheel.

I don't think of all the misery, but about the beauty that still remains.

ANNE FRANK

Love is incredible medicine. Spend the day with someone who makes your heart sing. Go for a walk together, enjoy a pot of tea or simply nestle into your couch and spend hours chatting. Human relationships can be the simplest and most beautiful tonic.

Becoming aware of your thoughts could mean giving them a name. Recognize that a consistent fear or nervousness could be anxiety, or a persistent inability to feel motivated can be a symptom of depression. Once you know where you stand, you know what you are working with.

Make eye contact during conversation. This shows that you are listening without judgement and allows you to focus on the present moment.

Remember that nothing can take away what you have learned through mindful meditation. When you are struggling, try to bring yourself home by using the skills you now hold.

Don't underestimate the value of Doing Nothing, of just going along, listening to all the things you can't hear, and not bothering.

A. A. MILNE

Take a blanket with you to the park today and spend time sitting in the grass. Find a visual point, such as a stray leaf or a blade of grass, and focus your gaze. Follow its movements as it catches the wind and remains still once again. This is one of life's simple pleasures. Feel the calm.

23

During your shower, make a special effort to feel the sensation of water against your skin. Notice the prickly, penetrating effect of the droplets and the warmth of the steam around your face. When your mind wanders, bring it back to the water.

••• 24 •••

Take notice of the world outside your door. Hear the kind voices of passing people, see the child holding their parent's hand, reach out and feel the feather that floats by. There is much beauty around if you look for it.

••• 25 •••

Before making a big decision, use your instinct and wisdom to think carefully about your path. Take as much time as you need to process the outcome before expressing your resolution.

••• 26 •••

Share childhood memories with a family member. Take joy in the little stories. This is a precious part of who you are.

As it's summer, pick somewhere outdoors to practise your mindfulness. Perhaps a grassy spot under a tree in the park or on the lawn in your garden. Establish this as your unique place to be mindful and return here each time you feel the desire, or need, to practise outside.

●●●(28)●●●

Improve your spinal health by practising the back bend. Stand up straight, keep your chest and heart lifted as you breathe deeply, in and out, and gently extend your head toward your lower back.

Go for a long walk during your lunch break. Aim for somewhere surrounded by greenery, if possible, and sit down in the sunshine for a short while.

Tell a family member about your mindful meditation practice and how it makes you feel.

If you have good thoughts they will shine out of your face like sunbeams and you will always look lovely.

ROALD DAHL

august

Perception of body image can change depending on our emotions. If you find yourself with negative thoughts regarding your body, use meditation to remind yourself that these thoughts are passing entities. Observe them, then let them go. Training your mind to engage less with these feelings is essential for self-love.

Increase your shoulder flexibility by standing with your left side against a wall and your left arm raised to the 12 o'clock position. Breathe in. Exhale as you lower your arm to the one o'clock position. Continue each hourly position, breathing in and out. Repeat on the right side.

••• 03 •••

Note down in your journal what you appreciate most in your life. What do you like about your character? Which of your morals cannot be compromised? Revert to this list when you're feeling uneasy to remind yourself of who you truly are.

••• 04 •••

Remember that self-care is a process. Carry out each practice without any expectations for the future – you are here, now, to experience calm and to find wisdom in a moment of difficulty.

••• 05 •••

[Meditation] lets you train your brain to be able to become more stable in an action-oriented way.

GOLDIE HAWN

●●● ●●●

If you feel anxious or worried, attempt to put your energy into something productive. Go for a walk or run, stretch your muscles in the gym, clean out the cupboard you have been meaning to rearrange, do some gardening, write in your journal.

●●● ●●●

Adopt an "always" approach. No matter how busy your day or if you forget to sit down for a session, you won't let the day end without practising mindful meditation. Even if it's for just a few minutes.

••• (08) •••

You are not the personification of your mind. By detaching yourself from your thoughts and feelings, you are improving your lived experience. For example, fearing a potential outcome shouldn't stop you from making an important decision. Recognizing this will free you from noxious emotions time and time again.

••• (09) •••

Become aware of the ground beneath your feet. Each step is another connection with our beautiful planet Earth.

••• (10) •••

Pause. Close your eyes and feel the beat of your heart. Count the beats, first to 20, then to 30, then 40. Open your eyes slowly and continue with your day.

Being "nice" and being "kind" are not the same thing. It's okay to say "no". Don't sacrifice being kind to yourself to be nice to someone else.

Make silence a part of your day. Switch off the noise around you by pausing for 20 minutes, allowing peace and quiet to fill your mind.

Once you begin to take note of the things you are grateful for, you lose sight of the things that you lack.

GERMANY KENT

Housework is a perfect time to practice mindful meditation. As you carry out your chores, bring your mind to the present moment — to the soap suds against your hands or the sound of the vacuum cleaner. Feel each sensation, listen to the sounds and inhale your surroundings.

With regular mindful meditation, you are making yourself the boss of your mind. Practise this by pulling your mind away from negative thoughts to focus on breathing.

Do not underestimate the power of doing very little. There is much therapy in pulling a blanket over you on the sofa and watching a film.

Listen to your body. Everything from tiredness and overwhelm to pain and anxiety is your body telling you to stop. You must allow some healing time. If you are feeling full of emotion, consider paying particular, and increased, attention to your breathing practice.

Spend time doing something you really enjoy. When you feel passionately about an activity and give it your full attention, your brain reaches what is called "a flowing state of mind" – where any regular feelings, from upset to body pains or mind chatter, dissipate as your thoughts are concentrated on the thing you love so much.

Fresh air can be a wonderful respite when you are feeling overwhelmed. Go outside to feel the air against your skin, the coolness against your eyes, your hair as it flows in the wind and the texture of the ground you are stepping on. Take deep breaths and allow your lungs to fill with that refreshing air.

While seated at your desk, take a deep, long breath in and let it out slowly. Repeat five times.

••• (21) •••

Nowhere can man find a quieter or more untroubled retreat than in his own soul.

MARCUS AURELIUS

When your emotions are competing for attention in your mind, give your concentration to only the most empowering voice. This is the one that is wise, in-tune with your instincts and speaks true to your heart.

•••(23)•••

Time with loved ones has never been more precious. Switch your phone off to avoid distractions and be present with them. Listen to every word, even if you disagree. Lead a wandering mind back to the activities you are enjoying together.

••• 24 •••

Write a list of what may go wrong today. Then, write a second list of what could go well. Study both and give each equal consideration. If you find yourself in a cycle of emotional negativity, this practice will help to train your mind to combat this.

••• 25 •••

Quiet helps to sharpen your senses. Choose to sit without the television or music and listen to the subtle noises of your home. Elevate your sense of mindfulness by contemplating how those sounds come to be.

••• 26 •••

The quality of your mind determines the quality of your life. Think of this as you meditate today.

Take a walk among the trees. Listen as the breeze whirls through the leaves and take in the dents and scars on each tree trunk you come across. Watch how they stand strong and tall, even in the wind, giving life to all creatures around them. Trees are wonderful.

•••(28)•••

Note down your core values and aim to activate one every day. Each evening, recap and celebrate how your values were have been practised.

•••(29)•••

What do you achieve from your worry? Think logically about the purpose of it. Worrying doesn't take away your troubles; however, it does take away your peace.

••• 30 •••

As you get used to meditating, let go of actively thinking. The key to deep meditation, where you feel an almost spiritual sensation, comes with time and with practice. Master the breathing exercises where you focus on the depth of your inhalation and exhalation, and combine them with sensual awareness, reaching that place of contentment will become second nature to you.

You do something you love, that makes you happy, and that gives you meditation.

ANGELINA JOLIE

september

If you aren't sure how best to respond to a toxic situation, simply do not respond at all. Allow any inevitable initial reactions and fallouts to occur, without becoming involved. As you reflect, use mindfulness and meditative techniques to find calm and patience. Write down how events are affecting you and use breathing exercises to help relieve distress or anxiety. Your instinct will eventually direct you toward a dignified solution.

Ease tension in your jaw muscles. Inhale deeply, scrunching your face at the same time. Exhale through an open mouth, dropping your jaw and extending your tongue.

As your mindful meditation sessions become longer, your transition back into daily life will also require more consideration. At the sound of your alarm, make slow movements to activate your fingers and toes, gently roll your shoulders and wind your neck carefully. When you're ready, gradually open your eyes. Factor this in when planning your day. Keep that feeling of peace with you as you begin your activities.

In every walk with nature one receives far more than he seeks.

JOHN MUIR

Look in the mirror and say, "I can cope with whatever comes my way." Repeat five times.

••• 06 •••

Dim the lights in your home after dinner to prepare your mind for sleep. This brings calm and a lowered sense of alertness to a setting and alleviates any loudness or tension.

••• 07 •••

Treat your mindful meditation sessions like essential exercise. While fitness routines are designed to train body muscles and keep them fit and healthy, practising the skills highlighted in this book is training the mind to keep it fit and healthy.

Maintaining boundaries is a form of self-conservation and self-kindness. It can be a challenge to honour those boundaries when you naturally prioritize loved ones, but to remain strong you must also protect yourself.

Dedicate one page of your journal to your most grounding mantra. Fill the blank space with the words that re-enforce your confidence and self-belief.

If possible, have yourself a device-free day. Leave your phone or laptop locked and enjoy the space this small gesture offers.

On particularly overwrought days, follow the practice of Progressive Muscle Relaxation. This involves tensing and releasing each of your muscles, in turn. Start from your face, neck and shoulders, then move on to your chest, abdomen, right arm, right hand, buttocks. Take your time to focus on each one. Continue with your left arm, left hand, before beginning on your lower body. Right leg, right foot, left leg, left foot.

Revitalize your home with colours or décor that promote relaxation and security – for example, a blanket in your favourite colour. Surround yourself with those elements, particularly in your corner of calm.

Life can be a challenge, and every one of us will feel pain during our lifetimes. Despite this, try to stay free of bitterness and stand by your principles.

Live each day better than the last. You may not be able to go back and fix what you are unhappy with, but you can start afresh today and move forward with confidence.

Meditation is a lifelong gift. It's something you can call on at any time.

PAUL McCARTNEY

Choose your response to actions that upset you. A calm and centred perspective can make all the difference to how you feel after the event and preserve relationships. Take a deep breath, sit with the feeling of discomfort while you discover how best to answer.

Listen to the comforting sounds of nature from your own bed or sofa each morning, by creating your own playlist or by using a mindfulness app.

••• 18 •••

What judgements and assumptions do you make when meeting a stranger? Take note of your preconceptions, letting your lesson be a less judgmental outlook.

Keep a mindful distance from those who gossip about you without truly knowing you or what you stand for. Social media allows anyone to speak their minds directly to you, but those words don't have to be absorbed.

Send a message of gratitude to a friend or family member today. Tell them how much you appreciate their influence or advice. Speak from your heart.

•••(21)•••

Consider making a shift from spending money on material possessions to investing in experiences. Perhaps skip your daily coffee and put the saving toward a weekend away. Imagine what could be learned and gained.

If you are struggling to fully relax, use the following mantra once you finish work each evening: "I allow myself to soften." Look in the mirror as you say it, repeating the phrase out loud every time you feel guilty for not doing more. This will help to reaffirm how it is you would like to feel.

••• (23) •••

Look how far your self-care has come in nine months. By trusting yourself to build a routine that is best for you, you are showing yourself self-trust.

••• •••

If you are feeling a little wobbly, give focus to the list of gratitudes you compile in the morning. Carry your journal with you, so you can remind yourself of the small things you are thankful for each day.

••• •••

A brief smile or "thank you" could be the kindness someone else needs to feel today.

••• 26 •••

When I meditate, there's something physical that actually happens, where I feel the neural pathways in my brain open up... and I feel my most sharp.

KATY PERRY

Declutter your space. Pack up clothes you no longer wear regularly, household items you barely notice and furnishings you have outgrown. Remember that someone else could make use of these items, so consider donating them to a local thrift store.

Run a hot bath, knowing this relaxation time is yours and yours alone. Allow your muscles to melt into the soothing warmth of the water. Close your eyes, inhale deeply and notice each muscle tingling in the heat as you exhale.

If public speaking or leading meetings causes you anxiety, look to your new-found coping skills to change how you feel. This is a situation you can make better by, for example, investing time with a self-confidence coach. By doing this, you are taking steps to alleviate your worry. Combine action with your regular mindful meditation practice for the best results.

I can end up just totally wacky, because I've made mountains out of molehills. With meditation, I can keep them as molehills.

RINGO STARR

october

Enduring or uncontrolled anger raises blood pressure, tightens muscles and releases adrenaline and cortisol hormones, activating the human "fight or flight" mechanism. Rather than stewing on a problem, examine the situation from a distance as though watching a film. When anger bubbles, slow your breath with long exhalations to keep your heart rate calm. Repeat until the anger passes.

Release emotional energy stored in your hips to reduce lower back pain. Lie on your back with your knees raised and feet flat on the ground. Inhale. Exhale and push your hips into the air. Hold for as long as is comfortable.

If you have not practised for a while but wish to continue your mindful meditation journey, start with the basic meditation tips at the beginning of this book. It won't take long to fall into the rhythm of more experienced exercises, but your mind muscles need to be stretched first. To reap the full effects of self-care, try to practise regularly and establish a routine once again.

One is never so strong as when one is broken.

HAZRAT INAYAT KHAN

••• **05** •••

Avoid repeatedly discussing a negative situation with friends. Instead, dedicate a few minutes to updating them, before moving on to a more positive and reflective conversation.

••• **06** •••

Sit comfortably with straight posture and allow your breath to slow to its natural rhythm. In your mind, scan each part of your body, from the top of your head down to your toes. Note the tingles, twitches, aches and tension. What sensations do you notice along the way?

Understand that you may have different coping strategies to others. While some people calm down by going for a run, others may wish to meditate or distract themselves by cooking a meal. Experiment with your own "coping toolkit" and embrace the activity that helps you most.

Everything you do is a choice. You are in control. Be present and enjoy your life choices.

··•(09)•··

Visualize each individual source of your stress being placed inside a balloon. Imagine taking that balloon to your window and letting it go. Watch it float away into the clouds. Let your worries go with it.

Reconnect with an old friend from whom you have drifted. Learn how their life has evolved since your last contact and fill them in on your life now. Make a face-to-face connection if possible, rather than using messages or social media.

Go for a long walk with a friend, but rather than talking to each other, walk in silence together. Share in the sights, smells and sounds of your environment in quiet contemplation. Later, compare what you each noticed. How did your perspectives differ?

Warming porridge is a comforting way to start an autumn day. By adjusting your meals to complement the season, you will continue to feel well in your body.

Be open to accepting help from close friends and allow them to check in on you.

In the end, just three things matter: how well we have lived. How well we have loved. How well we have learned to let go.

JACK KORNFIELD

Combat that hunched-over-a-laptop feeling. Lie face-down on the floor and bend your arms to make right angles. Keep your right hand on the ground as you roll onto your right side, so your right ear is on the floor. Then, lift your left leg and place your foot flat on the ground behind you. Feel the deep stretch in your shoulder. Repeat on your left side.

Reduce the impact of screen time on your everyday life by turning off pop-up phone or email notifications, only allowing alerts from loved ones. The others can be checked when, or if, you desire.

While it may be getting cooler outside, being out in nature is still wonderful therapy. Activities such as raking leaves, sweeping up garden matter and mowing the lawn can still be practised in the autumn and winter months. The aerobic effect will release endorphins and assist with stress relief.

Sit, with your journal, in quiet contemplation for ten minutes. Tune your ear to the sounds around you and note what you can hear.

You alone are enough. You have nothing to prove to anybody.

MAYA ANGELOU

Dedicate a morning to your self-care. Practise an extended mindful meditation session, incorporating both breathing and relaxation techniques. Jot down a list of 15 things from the summer months for which you are grateful. Make yourself a hot drink and bask in positivity.

●●● (21) ●●●

As the trees outside lose their leaves, introduce more greenery into your interior surroundings, both home and work. Potted plants absorb air pollutants and can be a soothing investment.

Alcohol can induce feelings of depression and anxiety — and also disturb sleep. Try to reduce your alcohol intake or opt for a small glass earlier on in the evening rather than just before bed.

As the clocks go back, invest in a selection of candles to give your home an ambient glow. Burn them as the early nights set in and create yourself the cosiest of settings.

Knowing yourself is the beginning of all wisdom.

ARISTOTLE

If the clouds allow, watch the sun rise. Write down in your journal the colour of the sky. You can repeat this once a week and note the changes as time passes.

Natural light promotes well-being and positivity, as well as increasing our alertness and productivity. During the autumn and winter months, consider swapping heavy curtains for blinds, or position mirrors so that more natural light is reflected around the room. Light walls will also enhance the brightness of a room.

Your opinions matter. Exchanging viewpoints is a healthy way to broaden your experiences. Take the initiative to ask questions and listen with genuine interest.

Have a digital declutter session by cleaning out old photos and videos from your phone. Organize and then let go with confidence.

••• 29 •••

If you're walking down the right path, and you're willing to keep walking, eventually you'll make progress.

BARACK OBAMA

••• (30) •••

While seated on chairs or at tables, place your feet flat on the floor to align your hips, rather than sitting cross-legged or with your knees folded. This position supports the rest of your body and assists with good posture.

Carve out a pumpkin for Halloween and place a candle inside for lighting. Use the flesh to create a hearty pumpkin pie or a deliciously warming spicy pumpkin soup. Read up on the history of the day and why pumpkins are used. Celebrating the meaning behind this date is a great way of focusing on the present.

november

Scientific research says sleep keeps us healthy by reducing stress levels and blood pressure, among other things. Prepare for a good quality night's sleep by giving your mind a rest. Try lying flat on your back in bed. Slow your breathing. Note where your body touches the bed, and in turn, begin "switching off" each body part, starting at your head.

Lie on your back and bring the soles of your feet together, with your knees out wide. Feel your hips opening up, freeing your muscles and stretching your inner thighs. Hold for as long as you can, breathing deeply.

Take delight in dancing in the rain, splash ferociously in puddles and catch any falling snowflakes in your mouth. Embrace winter like children do.

04

Close your eyes and breathe deeply. Imagine all the inspiration the universe has to offer coming toward you in a beam of light. Absorb the light into your mind, body and heart. Positivity and hope are yours if you want them.

05

Create a light and airy atmosphere around your home, and your mind, by pulling up the blinds and opening windows. It might be cold outside, but there is still natural light to be savoured.

Create a list of any non-essential items you plan to buy. Write them down, with the date next to it. Once 30 days have passed, ask yourself if you still need that item. If it's a no, cross it off the list. If yes, buy it.

••• 07 •••

Before bed, write down your greatest achievement of the day. Place the note on a bedside table, so as to remind yourself of your success in the morning.

Never be afraid to sit awhile and think.

LORRAINE HANSBERRY

Listen to the wild sounds of nature in wintertime — whether that's the rain beating against your window or the wind howling through the street. Acknowledge how they make you feel — good or bad. Give time to your thoughts for a minute or two. Then, let them pass.

••• (10) •••

Look in the mirror and with confidence, repeat the following mantra ten times: "I feel balanced and capable today." Breathe deeply between each sentence. Remember that affirmations and mantras can help manifest positivity.

Instead of watching television while you are on the treadmill, focus on the pace of your breathing and feel your lungs fill with air; notice how softly your feet land as you run or walk and the gentle movement of your arms.

When you reach home at the end of the day, remove your shoes and socks and take a seat. Once in a comfortable position, stretch, roll and flex your heels, toes and the arches of your feet – set them free and let them breathe.

If your intention is to practise yoga but you are feeling too exhausted, use the *Shavasana* or "corpse pose". This resting position, which involves lying on your back with your arms and legs stretched out, encourages deep relaxation.

Before bed, write down how you are feeling after your mindfulness exercises. In your notes, explain how these feelings helped or hindered you in your daily tasks.

•••• 15 ••••

There are no regrets in life, just lessons.

JENNIFER ANISTON

Place wind chimes outside your window. At night, when you hear them chime, settle into a comfortable position and find your place of calm.

Play soothing classical music as you drive. Imagine your spine growing in length, let your shoulders relax and loosen your grip on the wheel. Focus on where you are and the activity around you.

Anxiety does not empty tomorrow of its sorrows but only empties today of its strength.

CHARLES SPURGEON

As you wash the dishes, enjoy the warmth of the water as it trickles over your skin. Follow the gleaming bubbles as they pop, one by one, and listen to the gentle clinking of the dishes as you rinse and put them out to dry.

●●● (20) ●●●

If you're on a long train journey, don't wish away your time to your destination. Look out of the window and watch the varied landscapes that pass you by. There are new experiences to be had when you have a fresh perspective.

••• (21) •••

Look up at the clouds; notice the many shades of grey and the endless fluffy layers piling high into the sky. Witness their blanket-like texture and the pace at which they pass.

••• (22) •••

Take some time out to check in with your body – it is continually sharing its truth with you. Feelings of stiffness, dry skin, headaches or an uneasy tummy are signs that extra self-care is needed. Pay attention to your needs.

••• (23) •••

While hibernating from the cold, maintain your emotional and physical well-being by stretching your body indoors.

••• (24) •••

Recognize the triggers that take you backward on your journey of self-care. These may be found in a particular place; they could come from one person or specific conversation. Once you have established these, make a conscious choice to walk away from that bad energy with your head held high. Your mental health is most important.

••• (25) •••

Meditation is about getting still enough to know the difference between the voice and you.

OPRAH WINFREY

Kindness toward others goes hand in hand with kindness to oneself. Be sure to prioritize yourself, especially as social engagements increase during the festive season and schedules become more demanding. Factor some "me" time into your diary in the coming week.

••• (27) •••

Make an extra effort to visit friends at their home. The kindness of this simple gesture must not be underestimated, especially as the dark nights continue.

••• (28) •••

Spend some precious time alone. It gives you time to process your day, acknowledge your feelings, rest, and above all, enjoy *yourself*.

29

Invest in the items that bring you comfort, joy and security this winter. These may include soft woolly pyjamas and cozy blankets to wrap up in or spicy scented candles to enhance your surroundings. Allow yourself to be cosy and warm in your home — you deserve it. As the cold, dark nights draw in, surround yourself in that luxury, knowing you have the power to look after yourself.

30

If the world seems cold to you,
kindle fires to warm it.

LUCY LARCOM

december

01

Experiment with guided meditations. There are many books, apps and guided classes available on mindful meditation. The benefit is having an experienced instructor to help you to explore the inner workings of your mind. Unguided meditation, as described in this book, enables you to customize sessions to your lifestyle, but it requires commitment. Test out options to find the right medium for you.

02

Stimulate blood flow to the brain by practising the standing forward fold yoga position. Start standing with your arms high above your head. Inhale. As you fold from your hips, exhale until your palms are flat against the ground, bending your knees if needed.

The upcoming holiday season can bring reminders that we are truly blessed and privileged in our lives. Allow that appreciation to filter through you completely and acknowledge the position you hold on this day, in this year. Encompass those sentiments in your daily list of reasons to be grateful.

Make your own greeting cards for the festive season and include a heartfelt sentiment in each one. Think of the pure joy your efforts will bring your friends and family as they receive a keepsake from you that is wonderfully original.

••• (05) •••

Ask for a self-care day without feeling guilt. When you are overworked and overwhelmed, you are neither working nor resting. It is to your benefit, as well as to those around you, to return rested and productive once you have had time to heal.

••• (06) •••

You are your own person. You always have been and always will be. Do not measure yourself using someone else's ruler.

••• (07) •••

Whatever the present moment contains, accept it as if you had chosen it. Always work with it, not against it.

ECKHART TOLLE

If you wake up at night with whirring thoughts, lie flat on your back and breathe slowly, counting your breaths. Count "one" as you inhale, "two" as your exhale, "three" as you inhale, and so on. If you notice your mind wanders, redirect it to your breath. Continue the count until you drift off.

Precede every meal with a tall glass of water. With each sip, feel your body replenish and hydrate. Take a moment, while drinking, to be present in this action; notice the sensation of the water travelling down your throat and how revitalized you feel after.

••• (10) •••

Write down ten things you feel you have achieved this year through becoming more present and focused. Then note five things you feel need some work — for example, you may feel your concentration needs fine-tuning or you still struggle when handling conflict. These can be your focus in the new year.

••• (11) •••

Avoid caffeine, the stimulant found in coffee, non-herbal tea, fizzy drinks and chocolate, in the hours before bedtime. This will help settle your mind on the present moment, in time for sleep.

••• (12) •••

Take two minutes: sit down and slowly breathe in and out. Repeat.

Sort through your cupboards and pack up any winter coats, jackets, scarves, hats or gloves you haven't yet used this season. Take them to your nearest clothes bank today. Be thankful that you are able to help others who are less fortunate and could be struggling to keep warm.

●●● 14 ●●●

December can be busy, and it is more important than ever to dedicate time to your meditation sessions. Regardless of whether you do it for two minutes, five minutes or 20 minutes a day, frequent practice is what matters.

Keep a regular sleep schedule, even as festivities begin to take over.

Enjoy the season's foodie treats slowly and mindfully. Savour the flavours and fragrances.

A single act of kindness throws out roots in all directions, and the roots spring up and make new trees.

AMELIA EARHART

Swap cups of coffee for a more hydrating alternative. Feel your body replenish and soothe as you drink them. Mint or ginger will relax your stomach muscles, lemon refreshes you, while chamomile will unwind the mind.

••• 19 •••

Moderate physical activity such as yoga, running, fitness classes or weight training helps to combat insomnia. Pick an exercise you feel comfortable with whatever the weather and commit yourself to regular sessions.

••• 20 •••

During the deepest winter, be aware that this is a time for regeneration and relaxation. Life is prospering. Make the most of these quiet, reflective moments.

Closure comes from inside us, when we choose to accept the unfavourable thing that has happened to us. We may never understand why it happened, but we acknowledge it is a part of our journey. It is in the past, not our present.

••• 22 •••

According to a Zen proverb, you should sit in meditation for 20 minutes every day – unless you are too busy; then you should sit for an hour.

••• 23 •••

Listen to the people you interact with frequently. Pay attention to their words, rather than your interpretation of the conversation, and you will understand why they are who they are.

Pay particular attention to your mental health over the holidays. This time can be overwhelming, and you may need to practise more often than usual. Try hard to let your thoughts flow in and out of your mind, without showing an interest. Be a bystander in your own thought process.

Finding pleasure at home – whether in a family dinner or book club – can give us the strength to do incredible things.

REESE WITHERSPOON

••• 26 •••

Your body will always tell you what it needs. Sleep when you feel tired, eat when you feel hungry, meditate when you require healing.

••• 27 •••

Get a dose of natural light by taking a walk near home. Soak up the festive atmosphere of twinkling fairy lights and reindeer displays. Feel these symbols of joy lift your spirits.

••• 28 •••

Pause before assuming. Pause before judging. Pause before responding. Pausing before committing to a statement or action is an important way of keeping level-headed in any heated situation. Those brief few moments give you valuable time, making your response conscious and mindful.

Notice how your mindful meditation journey hasn't been about changing you as a person. It has been about learning to love yourself just as you are.

Mindful meditation doesn't have an expiry or completion date; it doesn't end with this book. View your journey much like exercise — as an ongoing form of self-care.

If you are brave enough to say goodbye, life will reward you with a new hello.

PAULO COELHO

conclusion

As you reach the end of this mindful meditation journey, I sincerely hope you feel fulfilled and proud of how much your mental and physical well-being has improved – and that you feel comfortable with the techniques that contribute toward a calm and happier mind. While mindfulness and meditation can improve mental health, please seek help from trained professionals if you feel you need more support. Now you have now completed the book, I hope you will continue to practise and reap the benefits of the deep-rooted wisdom and peace of mind you have found.

I wish you love, luck and everyday joy.

notes

Have you enjoyed this book?
If so, find us on Facebook at
Summersdale Publishers, on Twitter
at @Summersdale and on Instagram
at @summersdalebooks and get in
touch. We'd love to hear from you!

www.summersdale.com